GUMDROP BOOKS - Bethany, Missouri

STARTING SCIENCE

WEATHER

KAY DAVIES
AND
WENDY OLDFIELD

Steck-Vaughn
L I B R A R Y
A Division of Steck-Vaughn Company

Austin, Texas

Starting Science

Books in the series

Animals
Electricity and Magnetism
Floating and Sinking
Food

Light
Sound and Music
Waste
Weather

About This Book

This book will make children stop and think about different kinds of weather. It tells them about the effect weather has on our lifestyles, including the clothes we wear and the food we eat, as well as looking at how animals have adapted to it. Through the indoor and outdoor activities, it introduces children to methods of observing and recording the weather.

This book provides an introduction to methods in scientific inquiry and recording. The activities and investigations are designed to be straightforward but fun, and flexible according to the abilities of the children.

The main picture and its commentary may be taken as an introduction to the topic or as a focal point for further discussion. Each chapter can form a basis for extended topic work.

Teachers and parents will find that in using this book, they are reinforcing the other core subjects of language and mathematics. Through its topical approach **Weather** covers aspects of the following subjects: exploration of science, the variety of life, types and uses of materials, Earth and atmosphere, forces, energy and using light and electromagnetic radiation.

Editors: Cally Chambers, Susan Wilson

Typeset by Multifacit Graphics, Keyport, NJ
Printed in Italy by Rotolito Lombarda S.p.A., Milan
Bound in the U.S. by Lake Book, Melrose Park, IL
1 2 3 4 5 6 7 8 9 0 LB 96 95 94 93 92

Library of Congress
Cataloging-in-Publication Data

Davies, Kay.
    Weather / written by Kay Davies and Wendy Oldfield.
        p.   cm. — (Starting science)
    Includes bibliographical references (p. 31) and index.
    Summary: Text, illustrations, and suggested activities introduce weather, its effects on people and animals, and methods of observing and recording it.
    ISBN 0-8114-3007-3
    1. Weather — Juvenile literature. 2. Weather — Observers' manuals — Juvenile literature. [1. Weather — Experiments. 2. Experiments.] I. Oldfield, Wendy. II. Title. III. Series: Davies, Kay. Starting science.
QC981.3.D38 1992   91-30066
551.6—dc20   CIP AC

CONTENTS

The words that first appear in **bold** in the text or captions are explained in the glossary.

The weather can change very quickly. Rain clouds
and sunshine can be in the sky at the same time.

SUNSHINE AND SHOWERS

If you traveled around the world you would see many different kinds of weather.

Weather patterns are different around the world. **Climates** can change from one area to another.

Some countries stay very hot. Others are always cold. Some can be very dry and others have lots of rain.

Many countries have weather that changes from day to day and is different throughout the year.

Keep a weather diary for a few weeks to see how the weather changes.

	Monday	Tuesday	Wednesday	Thursday	Friday
Morning					
Afternoon					

Key					
Sun	Sun and cloud	Rain	Wind	Fog	Snow

Write in your diary at the same time every morning and every afternoon. The **key** will help you keep your records.

SPLISH-SPLASH

Rain can fall in a short shower or it can last all day.

Some rain sinks into the ground. It gives us plenty of water and helps plants grow.

Some water trickles into streams and rivers, and flows away to the sea.

Keep a graph of daily rainfall for a month.

Put a pail in a safe place where it can catch the rain.

Check it each morning for rainwater. Pour the water into a jar.

Cut a strip of paper to match the height of the water in the jar. Paste it on your rainfall graph.

Drops of rain fall from the sky. They collect in puddles
and make the roofs and pavements wet.

In bad weather, fishermen wear waterproof clothes.
These help keep out the sea water and the cold air.

KEEPING DRY

We need to wear special materials to keep us dry when it rains.

Animals and birds have oils in their fur and feathers.

This stops the water from reaching their skin.

Our clothes and shoes can be **waterproof**, too.

Get a piece of cotton fabric. Cut it into five small squares.

Cover four of them with nail polish, candle wax, glue, and furniture polish.

Put a few drops of water on each of the five squares.

Does the water soak through each one?

9

The greenhouse is hot and steamy.
It is a good place to grow plants from **tropical** countries.

TAKING THE TEMPERATURE

Temperature is a measure of how hot or cold things are.

We can guess the temperature of things just by feeling them. But to find out what the exact temperature is, we use a **thermometer**.

A thermometer is a thin glass tube with a colored liquid inside. Be careful when handling a thermometer, it can break easily.

When it warms up, the **liquid** rises up the tube. When it cools down, the liquid drops down again.

A **scale** of numbers on the tube tell what the temperature is.

Put a thermometer in some ice water. Then put it in some cool tap water.

What happens to the liquid in the tube?

Now gently hold the **bulb** of the thermometer.

Are your hands hot or cold? What is the temperature of your hands?

IT'S SUNNY TODAY

Do you know what causes night and day?

As the Earth turns, part of it faces the sun. Here it is daytime. On the other side, it is night.

Night   Day

The sun gives light and heat.

When you stand in the sunshine, your body makes a **shadow**. You can keep track of your shadow like this.

Mark a spot on the ground.

Stand on it and ask a friend to draw a chalk line around your shadow.

Do this early in the morning, at midday, and late in the afternoon.

How does your shadow change?

The sun makes us hot at the beach.
It is cooler in the shade of the umbrellas.

Ice cream is fun to eat on a hot day.
It makes you feel cool.

COOLING DOWN

The sun can burn your skin. It might even make you ill.

Covering your skin protects it from the sun and keeps you cool.

It is best to wear loose, thin clothes.

White or pale-colored clothes are cooler to wear than dark ones.

Cut two squares of felt — one black and one white.

Place them on a table in the sunshine. Put a thermometer under each.

Wait for half an hour.

What is the temperature under the two squares? Why is it hotter under the black square?

15

GUSTS AND GALES

We cannot see the wind.

But we can feel it. And we can watch it toss leaves in the streets and make flags flutter.

We can hear it. It whistles around doors and through branches.

You can test how strong the wind is.

Get pieces of tissue paper, newspaper, writing paper, wax paper, and thin and thick cardboard. Cut them all the same size.

Number them in order of thickness. Use string to tie them to a rope.

A light breeze will blow number one. A strong gust lifts all the numbers.

It is fun to fly a kite on a windy day.
The wind carries it high into the sky.

After a rainstorm the sun dries the land.
The wind blows the rising mist away.

DRYING UP

Heat from the sun changes rainwater into a gas. This gas is called **water vapor**. Sometimes we see it as fog.

Steam from a teakettle is water vapor.

It rises into the air just as water vapor rises in the sky.

Water vapor in the sky turns into clouds. Rain can fall from the clouds.

When the sun comes out after it rains, go outside with your friends. Ask each one to choose a puddle.

Draw chalk marks around your puddles. Come back every hour and make new chalk outlines.

Do the puddles change shape as they dry? Which one lasts the longest?

Sometimes dark, gray rain clouds cover the sky.
But other times clouds are as white and fluffy as cotton.

LOOK AT THE CLOUDS

Clouds make changing patterns in the sky. They are made of tiny drops of water which may fall as rain.

Mist swirling around our faces on a foggy day is really a low cloud.

If you feel your face or hair, it is damp where the mist has settled on you.

Mist settles on cobwebs and leaves, too.

Clouds are always moving across the sky.

Cover a sheet of black paper with clear plastic sheeting.
Lay it on the ground and watch the clouds in the reflection.
Hold up a strip of tissue paper to find the wind's direction.

Are the clouds moving the same way?

ICE AND SNOW

In cold weather, snowflakes can fall from the clouds.

Each snowflake has its own pattern.

Snowflakes are really tiny ice crystals.

When the air temperature is very cold, water in ponds and puddles freezes into ice.

Ice and snow do not melt until the air gets warmer.

Put three ice cubes on small plates for this test.

Put one back in the freezer, one on a sunny windowsill, and one in a cool room.

Check them often.

Which melts first?
Do they all melt?

Snow is fun to play with. We can press it together to make solid shapes like snowballs and snowmen.

The polar bear lives in the frozen lands of the **Arctic**.
Its thick fur keeps it warm.

WARM AND COZY

In cold weather, animals must keep warm to stay alive.

Seals have a thick layer of fat under their skin.

Birds puff out their feathers to trap warm air.

We dress in layers of thick clothes. They trap warm air around our bodies.

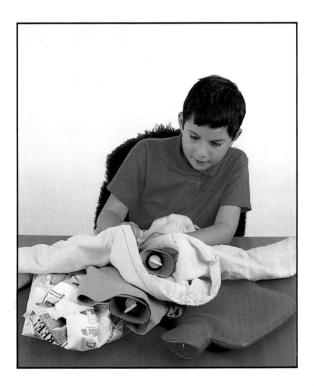

Fill four hot-water bottles with warm water.

Wrap one in newspaper, one in a coat, and one in a T-shirt. Leave the fourth one unwrapped.

After two hours take them out and feel them.

Which is the hottest? Which is the coldest?

USING THE WIND

The force of the wind can push a sailboat.

Wind can be used to turn the blades of a windmill for pumping water, grinding corn, or making electricity.

You can make your own windmill.

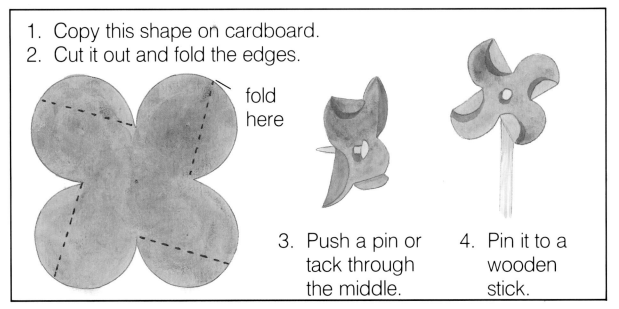

1. Copy this shape on cardboard.
2. Cut it out and fold the edges.

fold here

3. Push a pin or tack through the middle.

4. Pin it to a wooden stick.

Blow on your windmill to make sure it turns freely.

Take your windmill outside on a windy day.
Watch it spin faster when a gust comes along.

The hot-air balloon rises high up and the wind blows it across the sky.

Satellites take pictures of our weather from space.
Scientists can forecast changes in the weather.

HOW'S THE WEATHER?

Scientists collect information and make weather forecasts for television, radio, and newspapers.

The forecasts can help us decide what clothes to wear.

We can tell if it will be good weather for a picnic or cloudy and raining.

Sometimes we can forecast the weather by looking at the clouds and their shapes.

What type of clouds can you see out the window?

Fair weather

Rain

Thunder

Night

= Good weather

Morning

= Bad weather

Ask people if they know any local weather sayings.

Make them into a book.

Test them to see if they are true.

Can you guess what this saying tells us?

GLOSSARY

Arctic Frozen lands at the most northern part of the Earth.

Bulb The rounded base of a thermometer which holds the liquid.

Climate The kind of weather a place has throughout a year.

Key Pictures that tell you what the chart or map means.

Liquid A runny substance, like water or mercury.

Satellite A machine sent into space to travel around the Earth.

Scale A series of numbers.

Shadow A dark patch of shade made when an object blocks out light.

Temperature An exact measurement of how hot or cold something is.

Thermometer An instrument for measuring temperature.

Tropical A tropical climate is hot and steamy.

Waterproof Material that water can't pass through.

Water vapor The gas formed when water evaporates.

Weather patterns Changes in the weather which happen regularly through the year.

FINDING OUT MORE

Books to read:

Air, Water, Weather by Michael Pollard (Facts on File, 1987)
How Weather Works "My First Reference Library" series (Gareth Stevens, 1991)
I Can Be a Weather Forecaster by Claire Martin, "I Can Be" series
  (Childrens Press, 1987)
It's Raining Cats and Dogs: All Kinds of Weather and Why We Have It
  by Franklyn M. Branley (Houghton Mifflin, 1987)
Let's Look at Sunshine by Constance Milburn (Franklin Watts, 1988)
Snow is Falling by Franklyn M. Branley (Harper & Row Junior Books, 1985)
Weather (Price/Stern/Sloan, 1987)
Weather and Climate, "Gareth Stevens Information Library" (Gareth Stevens)
Weather Watch by Adam Ford (Lothrop, Lee & Shepard, 1983)

PICTURE ACKNOWLEDGMENTS

Bruce Coleman Ltd. 22 (Kage); Chapel Studios 10; Eye Ubiquitous 13, 19 top;
©Michael Keller/FPG cover; Oxford Scientific Films 18; PHOTRI 16 top, 20, 27;
TRH 28; Topham 8, 14, 21 top; Wayland Picture Library 7, 15 top, the following
commissioned from Chapel Studios (Zul Mukhida) 6 bottom, 9, 11, 12, 15 bottom,
16 bottom, 19 bottom, 21 bottom, 25; ZEFA 4, 6 top, 12, 23, 24, 26.
Artwork illustrations by Rebecca Archer. Cover design by Angela Hicks.

INDEX

First published in 1990 by Wayland
(Publishers) Ltd.
©Copyright 1990 Wayland (Publishers) Ltd.